Contents

Words shown in **bold** in the text are explained in the glossary.

All the places in this book are shown on the map on page 22.

How Do We Get Around?

In cities, some people drive small electric cars.

When these cars are parked, they can be plugged in and recharged.

In Guatemala, many people travel from village to village on brightly painted buses.

People and goods are sometimes carried by oxcarts in Myanmar.

Hitching a ride on Mum in Vietnam!

In snowy Mongolia, some people travel by reindeer.

It's all aboard for this family in Colombia.

All Aboard the School Bus

From Monday to Friday, yellow school buses can be seen on roads across the United States and Canada.

Each morning, about 30 million children climb aboard these yellow buses.

It takes 500,000 buses and drivers to get that many children to school every day!

A yellow school bus from 1927

The bright yellow colour of school buses can easily be seen in rain, snow and fog, and when there's not much light. Making school buses easy to see helps keep children safe.

A Pedal Power School Bus

On the crowded streets of Delhi in India, many people travel in **rickshaws**.

A rickshaw is pulled by a driver on foot or riding a bicycle.

A rickshaw

Some children travel to school in rickshaws.

This rickshaw school bus carries up to 10 children. Their backpacks ride on the roof.

A rickshaw school bus

For many children, the journey to school can take two hours!

Off to School by Canoe

Every morning, canoes filled with school children set off across a **lagoon** near the city of Lagos, in Nigeria.

The children live in fishing villages on one side of the lagoon.

Their school is on the other side of the lagoon.

The older kids paddle the canoes, while their younger friends enjoy the ride to school.

When the children return home from school, their fathers use the canoes to go fishing on the lagoon.

A fisherman on the lagoon

Animal Power

People have travelled by horse and donkey power for about 5000 years.

Horses and donkeys were originally wild animals.

A donkey cart carrying cans of water in Botswana

A horse and cart in Tibet

Over time, our **ancestors** tamed and trained them.

A sled dog team

In Greenland, Inuit people have travelled by dog sled for thousands of years. Each dog in a team can pull one and a half times its own weight over the snow and ice.

Snowmobiles

In many snowy places around the world, dog sleds have been replaced by snowmobiles.

Snowmobiles are often used just for fun.

In Norway, Sami reindeer **herders** live alongside their animals.

The large herds of reindeer move from place to place to find food.

The herders ride alongside on snowmobiles.

Sami people describe themselves as 'reindeer walkers'. That's because they used to walk or ski for hundreds of kilometres alongside their reindeer herds.

A tired baby reindeer riding on a snowmobile

A Sami herder with his reindeer

Taking the Train

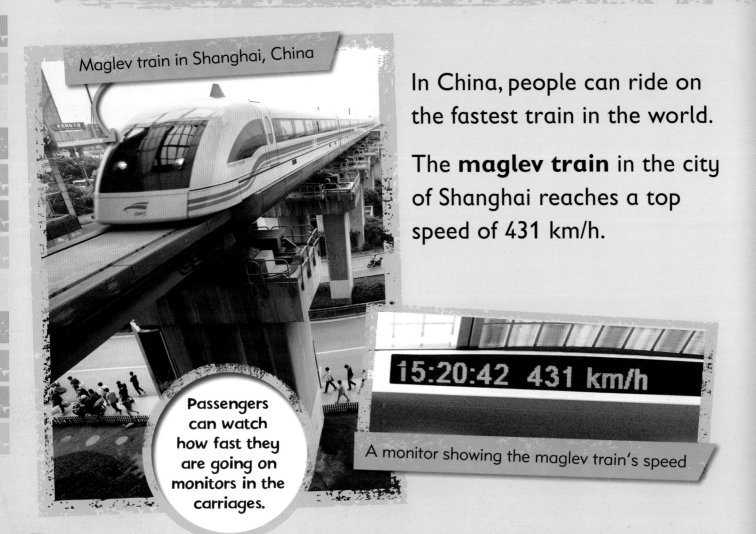

Maglev train in Shanghai, China

Passengers can watch how fast they are going on monitors in the carriages.

15:20:42 431 km/h

A monitor showing the maglev train's speed

In China, people can ride on the fastest train in the world.

The **maglev train** in the city of Shanghai reaches a top speed of 431 km/h.

This train in Bangladesh is crowded with people travelling to see their families for the Eid-ul-Adha festival.

Flying Doctors

In the **outback** of Australia, many people live hundreds of kilometres from a doctor or hospital.

When people need help, doctors come to them by plane.

A flying doctor might operate on a patient inside the plane.

Sometimes the plane acts like a flying ambulance and carries a patient to the nearest hospital.

The flying doctors' planes often have to land on rough ground where there is no runway. At night, people waiting for the doctor use their car headlights to show the plane where to land.

A flying doctors' plane

Walking All the Way

Children all over the world get to school by walking.

These boys in Uganda are walking to school.

They are bringing chairs from their homes with them.

Many children in the UK get to school in a walking bus. Long lines of children and several adults walk around town collecting children from each street.

A walking bus

21

Where in the World?

Greenland
Page 13

United Kingdom
Page 21

Belgium
Page 4

Norway
Pages 14–15

Tibet, China
Page 12

Mongolia
Page 5

China
Page 16

North America

Europe

Asia

United States and
Canada Pages 6–7

Nigeria
Pages 10–11

Africa

Vietnam
Page 5

South America

Australia

India
Pages 8–9

Guatemala
Page 4

Colombia
Page 5

Botswana
Page 12

Uganda
Page 20

Bangladesh
Page 17

Myanmar
Page 5

Australia
Pages 18–19

Glossary

ancestor
A relative who lived a long time ago. For example, your great-grandparents are your ancestors.

herder
A person who herds, or moves, animals from place to place so that the animals can find food.

lagoon
A shallow lake or pool of saltwater that is connected to the ocean.

maglev train
A train that uses magnets called electromagnets to move at high speed. The magnets also lift the train so it floats slightly above the rail.

outback
A vast, desert-like area of Australia where very few people live.

rickshaw
A small, two-wheeled carriage or other vehicle that is pulled by a person on foot or on a bicycle.

Index

Learn More Online

To learn more about
travel around the world, go to
www.rubytuesdaybooks.com/getaround